# ROCKY MOUNTAIN ROMANCE

# ROCKY MOUNTAIN ROMANCE

### The Life and Adventures of Catharine and Peter Whyte

**BIOGRAPHY/ROMANCE**

## by Kim Mayberry

PUBLISHED BY ALTITUDE PUBLISHING CANADA LTD.
1500 Railway Avenue, Canmore, Alberta T1W 1P6
www.altitudepublishing.com
1-800-957-6888

Extreme care has been taken to ensure that all information presented in
this book is accurate and up to date. Neither the author nor the
publisher can be held responsible for any errors.

Publisher    Stephen Hutchings
Associate Publisher    Kara Turner
Editors    Lauri Seidlitz, Jennifer Nault

We acknowledge the financial support of the Government
of Canada through the Book Publishing Industry Development
Program (BPIDP) for our publishing activities.

**Altitude GreenTree Program**
Altitude Publishing will plant twice as many trees as were used
in the manufacturing of this product.

**National Library of Canada Cataloguing in Publication Data**
Mayberry, Kim
   Rocky Mountain Romance : the life and adventures of Catharine and
Peter Whyte / Kim Mayberry.

(Amazing stories)
Includes bibliographical references.
ISBN 1-55153-998-5

1. Whyte, Peter, 1905-1964. 2. Whyte, Catharine Robb, 1906-1979. 3.
Rocky Mountains, Canadian (B.C. and Alta)--Biography. 4. Painters--
Canada--Biography. I. Title. II. Series: Amazing stories (Canmore, Alta.)
ND249.W53M39 2003    759.11    C2003-910170-3

An application for the trademark for Amazing Stories™
has been made and the registered trademark is pending.

Printed and bound in Canada by Friesens
2 4 6 8 9 7 5 3 1

The front cover shows Catharine and Peter Whyte camping ca. 1930.
All photographs are reproduced courtesy of the
Whyte Museum of the Canadian Rockies.

For Kevin

Peter and Catharine Whyte outside their home in Banff ca. 1935

# Contents

# Prologue

*The Rocky Mountains cut a jagged horizon in front of Peter and Catharine Whyte. The newlyweds placed their easels a few metres apart, rejoicing in the grandness of their surroundings. A temperate breeze mixed the smell of budding saplings with the artist's oil paints, fluttering the pages of their sketchbooks. Comfortable in this alpine setting, Peter adeptly traced an outline of a familiar mountain face. Glancing over at her, he smiled as he watched his new bride busy painting. He had longed to share these mountains with her. Finally, she was here!*

*Adapting to her new setting, Catharine rushed to capture the beauty before her. The clouds fleeted overhead. Shadows loomed then lifted. The sun shone amber then bright white. Conditions varied so quickly. In her mind, she drew parallels to the flurry of changes she'd experienced since leaving Boston. Her life would never be the same again.*

# Chapter 1
# Catharine: A Debutante's Life

**S**parkles of bright light glinted from hanging crystal chandeliers in the ballroom of Boston's Hotel Somerset. It was December 8, 1924, and more than 1000 of the East Coast's most prosperous and well-known people, dressed in their finest evening attire, had gathered to welcome the newest wave of society princesses. At the tender age of 18, a demure and somewhat nervous Catharine Robb made her social debut. Her bobbed, brown hair was slightly wavy and her flapper-style dress hid her slender physique.

Months of preparation had led to this moment in the spotlight as Catharine walked to the front of the room for her formal introduction to the large crowd.

For months before this night, the debutantes were caught up in a flurry of activity. They cavorted at luncheons, sipped tea at dozens of tea parties, waltzed at dances, and mingled at pre-parties. The girls also performed charity work to demonstrate their ability to continue their family's history of gracious benevolence. In the days preceding the event, heaps of packages arrived at Catharine's house containing expensive gifts from some of the wealthiest people in America. Meanwhile, Catharine and the other debutantes were pampered. They enjoyed manicures, had their hair cut and styled according to the latest fashion, and shopped for the perfect dress and accessories to ensure they looked their best when they came out. All eyes would be on them at the debutantes' ball in Boston.

Members of Bostson's society memorized Emily Post's etiquette guidelines. Etiquette demanded attention to detail and poised participation. People were very concerned about how others perceived them, while at the same time cultivating strong perceptions of others. Polite gossip was not only acceptable, it was a way of keeping others in line.

Hushed rumours swirled around social circles — and Catharine would soon find herself in the centre.

**Dear Diary**

In the midst of the whirl of events of her debutante year, Catharine turned to her journal to confide her anxiety about coming out. She would later reveal that she took part in the debutante events more to please her father and brother than out of her own desire. She disliked being the centre of attention, and her heart pounded at the thought of it. She felt much more comfortable talking face to face with people so she could listen attentively and let the conversation focus on them.

In her journal, Catharine could bare her soul and escape a world where niceties and politeness mattered more than expressing oneself. It was a secret place where she could confide her true feelings and write things that she would never tell others. She began writing regularly during her adolescent years beginning each entry "Dear Buz." She signed off as "Katrinka." Imaginary names provided a vehicle for candidness. In her journal, Catharine expounded on daily occurrences, contemplated life's bigger questions, and poured out her feelings.

Catharine's very first journal entries were the

scrawled observations of an 11-year old. These first musings paint a picture of a happy childhood. She frankly details her dislike of certain school subjects and how she hates to be told what to do. Her entries are like those of any child.

However, even as a young girl, her life was anything but ordinary. Catharine enjoyed many cultural experiences not available to other children. Growing up, she was taken to lectures, plays, art galleries, and museum exhibits. She was enrolled in drama, music, and art lessons. Her parents encouraged learning, creativity, and a well-rounded personality.

She came from diligent stock. Intelligent and skilled, Catharine's family members had all worked hard to attain the finer things in life. Her family felt it was important to continue to strive and achieve, while helping others along the way. She was expected to do the same.

**Scholars, Engineers, and Artists**
Some people called Catharine's grandfather, Edward Sylvester Morse, a genius. He was a student of the well-known naturalist Louis Agassiz at Harvard College. In school, Edward's interests were focussed on the natural world, and he voraciously learned about the marine habitat of the East Coast where he

grew up. Later, he would become the first director of the Peabody Museum in Salem, Massachusetts, which featured biological, anthropological, and marine collections. Edward's scientific mind was accompanied by a deep interest in people. His curiosity about other cultures took him to Japan in the late 1800s, where he became one of the first Americans to explore a country that was wary of Western influence. Edward submerged himself in the artistry of Japanese culture. He wandered the country collecting pottery, ceramics, and other fine examples of Japanese craftsmanship. The treasures he gathered would accumulate into a priceless collection of artifacts.

After her grandfather's death in 1925, Catharine and her mother spent hours cleaning out his house. Amid the usual household clutter were scraps of notes with scrawls such as "Meet me at four," notebooks crowded with writing, piles of well-used books, dusty boxes containing props for lectures, scientific papers, correspondence, and a jar of monkey bones. It was an eclectic assortment, well kept and logically ordered, reflecting his wide-ranging interests.

Sorting through her grandfather's collection sparked Catharine's interest in the world beyond Boston. Flicking through old photographs from

Japan, she noted the sparse elements of Zen interior design, elegantly crafted pottery, and images of her grandfather with Japanese royalty. Sitting in the midst of her grandfather's things, Catharine dreamt of travelling the world and exploring exotic places, collecting treasures of her own along the way.

## A Bright Protégé

Edward Sylvester Morse was lecturing in Dubuque, Iowa, when he met a young orphan named Russell Robb. Peering over the lectern, Edward was encouraged by the sight of young Russell, sitting up straight, intent on every word. After the lecture, the boy boldly approached Edward. Russell's questions were intelligent and the two began conversing. Upon hearing that Russell had lost both his parents and had an uncertain future, Edward decided to help the young man.

At 14 years of age, Russell Robb had been forced to leave school and work as an errand boy. His mind craved intellectual stimulation, so he attended any free lecture he could fit in around his work schedule. He was a bright boy with an inquiring mind.

Edward arranged for Russell's guardians to send him to school. Later, Edward found Russell a summer job in Boston to help with the cost of school tuition.

After only one year of high-school training, his protégé attended the Massachusetts Institute of Technology, studying electrical engineering. After graduation, he quickly rose to senior vice-president and treasurer of Stone and Webster, a successful engineering firm. Edward Sylvester Morse and Russell Robb became like father and son. They appreciated each other's talents and personalities. Russell's soft-spoken demeanour and focussed drive also won the affection of Edith Morse, his mentor's daughter and a businesswoman and artist in her own right. Together with a girl friend, Edith drew on her education at the Boston School Museum of Fine Arts, to run an embroidery design company. Edith gave up her business after she married Russell in 1898.

**An Idyllic Childhood**
Russell and Edith Morse Robb mixed a passion for learning and culture with their keen aptitude for business. They wisely invested their money and were able to afford many of life's finer luxuries. The Robbs' first child, Russell Jr., was born on November 13, 1901. Their daughter, Catharine, was born five years later on June 13, 1906.

The Robb house was a stately, white structure located on acres of rolling land just outside Concord,

Massachusetts. Sturdy roman pillars marked either side of the main entrance. Trees, pathways, flower-beds, and trellises intersected the well-kept lawn. The overall effect of the estate was one of tasteful elegance. The interior of the home mirrored this refined style. The grandness was most evident in the details: ivory walls, arched doorways, crown mouldings, and graceful Victorian décor.

Catharine's parents provided well for their children. Russell Robb Sr. was his daughter's idol. A gentle leader who cared deeply about his family, he ensured his children received the finest in education and experience. Like many younger sisters, Catharine also looked up to her older brother. Tussling with her brother, Catharine grew tough and comfortable in the company of men. From playing sports on the back lawn to sharing advice, their relationship was founded on mutual respect and a shared sense of humour.

Jean Caird, Catharine and Russell's nanny, was close to the children. She was a strong Scottish woman with snowy white hair tucked neatly in a bun. She remained part of the Robb household even after the children were gone. Jean could be strict, but was more often a confidante to Catharine. She eased Catharine's worries about the pressures the young woman faced as a debutante, but reminded her of her duty to live a life that benefited others. It was Jean who guided Catharine's progression from a carefree child to a proper young lady.

## A Proper Young Lady's Education

Part of being a proper young lady was attending boarding school. Catharine was enrolled at the Mary C. Wheeler School in Providence, Rhode Island, from 1921 to 1924. Wheeler was an all-girls school, complete with dress code and strict anti-fraternizing policies. The school provided its students with a well-rounded learning environment. It boasted well-equipped classrooms, first-rate teachers, and many extra-curricular activities. Catering to the East Coast's wealthy elite, Wheeler had a reputation to uphold.

Students were expected to be on their best behaviour at all times. Administrators frequently examined letters to ensure students were receiving mail only from relatives and family friends — not secret boyfriends. One girl was expelled from the school for deliberately giving her chaperone the slip so that she could meet her beau.

Catharine was an obedient and conscientious

student. She belonged to the School Spirit Board, the Athletic Board, and the House Committee. Called "Robbie" or "Kay" by her friends, Catharine was comfortable in the school environment and was a popular student who enjoyed spending time with her friends.

**First Love**

Every summer, Catharine's family vacationed in Seal Harbor, Maine, where some of America's wealthiest families congregated. Regular visitors included the Rockefellers, the wealthiest family in America. Catharine made friends with the two eldest sons, Nelson and John Davidson Rockefeller III whose politeness and gentle manners attracted her. Catharine appreciated the Rockefellers' gracious refinement and was entranced by the lavishness of their lifestyle. The Robbs were wealthy, but their lifestyle was not nearly as extravagant, and the time Catharine spent with the Rockefellers was very special.

Away from the hustle and bustle of the city, the Rockefellers and the Robbs enjoyed warm, carefree days in their summer resort haven. As their families socialized, Catharine and John spent more and more time together. In the afternoons, the two enjoyed sailing trips along the rocky coast. In the evenings, there were dinners, dances, and relaxing hours spent around driftwood fires on the beach.

During her teenage years, Catharine eagerly anticipated her summers with John. Throughout the rest of the year, they wrote letters to each other, and at Christmas, he sent her gifts, such as a 14-carat gold pen and Origan de Coté perfume. Catharine had begun to care deeply for John and believed the feeling was mutual. Then came the summer when her life's path took a different turn.

\* \* \*

Jazzy music wafted out the dance hall's doors, which had been propped open to let in the cool night air. As Catharine climbed the steps, her stomach flip-flopped. It had been more than a year since she had seen John and she was nervous about seeing him again. She had imagined the two of them dancing the night away. She walked into the dance hall and spied John. Her heart sank. She could see him, debonair as usual, but he did not seem to notice her. Catharine took a seat and waited. Eventually John made his way over, but after saying a quick hello, he was off again. They didn't share a single dance.

## Chapter 2
# Peter: A Mountain Man

T he sun rose between two mountain peaks, casting a pink glow over stands of evergreen trees and reflecting off the rippling surface of the Bow River far below. Peter Whyte sat precariously on a rounded stone that jutted out from the cliff at just the right angle to afford a panoramic view of the valley he was sketching. His supplies were laid out close by, in a natural pocket in the rock.

Peter had left the buzzing centre of Banff in the heart of the Canadian Rockies early that morning. He wanted to spend some time alone, away from school, and the store. This perch was his favourite place. Fresh air, a pencil, paper, paints, and a canvas: what more could a person need? Peter rolled up his sleeves and set to work.

## The Lure of the Rockies

Peter's grandfather had felt the lure of the Canadian Rockies while living far away in Airdrie, Scotland. When John Donaldson Curren's wife passed away, leaving him with a son and three-year old daughter, Annie, he started packing. He believed that Canada could offer them a better life, and he wanted to put some distance between himself and his sad memories.

The trio sailed over the rough Atlantic Ocean bound for the east coast of North America, and then travelled onward to Alberta. Nestled at the base of the distinctive Cascade Mountain, a short distance northeast of Banff, was a small mining village called Anthracite. Fewer than 100 people were living in the area in 1886 when the single-parent family finally arrived, exhausted from their journey. Although remote and sparsely populated, this is where John Donaldson Curren set down his bags to build himself and his family a new life.

Around the same time, the Rocky Mountains

also beckoned a young upstart named Dave McIntosh Whyte. Looking for adventure and a chance to prove himself, Dave left Nash Creek, New Brunswick, and took a job working as a section man for the Canadian Pacific Railway, near Banff. For eight years he worked diligently for the CPR and quickly moved up the ranks to section foreman. He made a name for himself in the Bow Valley as a hard worker and a good friend. He made an especially strong impression on a young woman from Anthracite.

In 1901, Dave Whyte and Annie Curren were married. A year later they had their first child, Cliff, then a daughter named Lila, and sons Peter and Dave (called Jack) soon followed. The children were raised in a strict Scottish Presbyterian home.

The Whyte family was one of the original families to settle in the burgeoning community of Banff. Dave was an astute businessman. He soon saved enough money to buy several properties in Banff, a town that was becoming increasingly popular as a tourist destination.

**The Park Store**
The spelling of the family name has been a topic of contention and a source of confusion ever since Dave

Whyte opened Banff's first general store, the Park Store, in 1894. He sold dry goods and supplies to the mining families, CPR workers, and the trickle of wealthy tourists who visited the area. To advertise the store, Dave decided he would need a large sign to encourage passers-by into his establishment.

So Dave hired a painter. The painter assumed the family name was spelled with an "i" rather than the "y" Dave preferred. When Dave returned from a business trip, there was his sign, gleaming brightly with the misspelling. Because of the cost to correct the error, and since he felt his surname would more than likely be mistaken for this spelling anyway, Dave adopted the "i" with an easygoing nod. From that point on, individual family members could choose their preferred spelling. Peter chose the "y" appellation at the beginning of his painting career, a spelling he felt was more aesthetically pleasing.

**Enduring Friendships**

Unlike most settlers in the area, Dave White got to know the Native peoples who lived about 65 kilometres east of Banff on the Morley Reservation. For generations, members of the Stoney band had used an ancient hunting trail that took them right past Dave's Sawback Section House. This was the spot where the

Stoneys forded the Bow River. Looking for a place to rest after crossing the river, the Stoneys often stopped at Dave's cabin. Eager for company, Dave and his friends would swap stories. A love of storytelling and mutual respect cemented a relationship between the White family and the Stoneys.

Dave and Annie White's children grew up visiting with Stoney families. Moreover, one Stoney man, Mark Poucette, became particularly close to the White boys. Peter explained, "All his boys are dead, so he adopted my brothers and myself as his sons and always called us his own. Today he took great delight in telling some friends I was his son, explaining how he had known me since I was born and how my brothers and I were Stonies."

**Early Adventures**

A middle child, born January 22, 1905, Peter found ways to get the attention of his parents. He had a penchant for running off on his own and often left home without telling anyone where he was going. One day his independent spirit got the better of him. He clambered into the back of a covered vehicle and was transported to the edge of town before the driver spotted the stowaway. When he was returned to his alarmed parents, Peter received a spanking as punishment.

## Peter: A Mountain Man

Peter's adventurous nature meant he was one of the first in Banff to try the latest craze sweeping the nation: skiing. Skis were introduced to Banff by visiting Scandinavians in the early 1900s. Until then, snowshoes were the preferred method of back-country winter transportation. Before long, skis grew in popularity and "ski running" became a handy way of getting around. Acquiring skis was expensive, so Peter and his friends fashioned themselves makeshift pairs from spliced toboggans or planks of wood. They looped leather straps around their boots to bind the contraptions to their feet. Eventually, they saved up enough money to buy real wooden skis and explored a large territory around Banff. The base of nearby Mount Norquay became a favourite spot for downhill exploits. As teenagers, Peter, his brothers, and his friends were the first recreational skiers in Banff. They founded the town's first skiing organization, the Banff Ski Club, in the early 1920s.

Much to his parents' dismay, ski jumping captured Peter's fancy when he was 15 years old. At first, Peter and his friends jumped off the roof of a friend's house onto mounds of snow they had shovelled below to cushion the landing. They progressed to building jumps out of scraps of lumber. The boys spent days searching for leftover lumber, carting it to a suitable location, constructing a "J"-shaped structure to leap from, and then gleefully whizzing down the slope and sailing into the air in a stiff, straight Nordic position. Peter became one of the best jumpers in the region.

Skiing was Peter's winter passion. The rest of the year he participated in team sports and enjoyed hiking and horseback riding with friends. He felt at ease in his mountain setting, often hiking deep into the back country. His love for the region went beyond the activities he pursued. The landscape engaged his spirit and captured his imagination. He could spend hours gazing at the jagged peaks, watching the curls of clouds float past. He loved the aroma of pine needles and the crisp alpine air.

**Banff's First Local Artist**
Peter's first-hand knowledge of the area inspired a love of drawing. He was fascinated by how he was able to recreate in his sketchbook the rugged beauty of the mountains and the larch-filled valleys he so loved to explore.

To develop his artistic skills, Peter enrolled himself in a correspondence cartooning class. Sending away for the instruction kit was very exciting — receiving a package in the mail was even more so. A keen, sensitive observer, Peter was a quick study. His talent blossomed by rigorously following the models given in the course and through hours of practice. In his lifetime, Peter made thousands of quickly rendered, often humorous, sketches. Later, his talents expanded to photography.

Not surprisingly, Peter's favourite subject in school was art. One of his first art teachers was Nora Drummond-Davis. Nora was an eccentric woman who lived with 11 dogs and hordes of cats in a tiny cabin on the outskirts of Banff. She made her living illustrating postcards and painting wildlife and nature canvases that were displayed in some of Banff's hotels and businesses. Each week she would mount her horse and ride to the Banff school. Even though the other students thought Ms. Drummond-Davis smelled like her animals, Peter eagerly sat close to his teacher as she guided his natural talent.

Other than art class, Peter found little enjoyment in school. Technically, he did not graduate, although he did manage to obtain a high school diploma. Even though he had dropped out of school in Grade 11, the school administration asked Peter to complete the ink drawings that adorned the diplomas of each graduate. Since there was an extra document, and feeling that he deserved something in return for his excellent work, Peter prepared himself a diploma.

After he left school, Peter worked for the Brewster Transport Company. He had a good relationship with his employers and worked for them on and off for many years. Peter's various positions included driving buses and cars, guiding tourists, and training Brewster Transport Company staff. He chauffeured many wealthy and powerful people. Politicians, royalty, and Hollywood film stars all visited the area. Not intimidated by wealth, Peter got to know some of the movie stars and even taught Lillian Rich to ski. He acted as an extra in some of the films that were shot on location in the Rockies. Between shifts, he tried to spend as much time as possible drawing, painting, and sketching.

Peter would often wander off on his own, find a comfortable patch of grass, and set to work sketching his surroundings. The talent evident in his art captured the attention of many of the visiting artists who were drawn to Banff's beautiful landscape. Peter found himself acting as a guide and painting partner to many of these professional artists.

Belmore Browne was a prominent artist who lived in Banff for 19 years. An avid outdoor enthusiast and alpinist, Belmore was grateful to take advantage of Peter's local knowledge and Peter was equally pleased to learn painting techniques from the accomplished artist. Peter took private lessons from Belmore. Prompted by Belmore Browne's suggestion — and wanting to explore the glamorous Hollywood Hills — Peter decided to attend the Otis Art Institute in Los Angeles.

His family was not enthusiastic about Peter's budding career as an artist. It did not seem to be a very lucrative lifestyle. They would have preferred him to have chosen a more sensible career. Despite a lack of support, Peter followed through with his decision to study far from home.

His work with Brewster had given Peter the travel bug, which complemented his independent streak. To earn money for school, he set off on his own to work on board the S. S. *Manchuria,* a ship that cruised from New York to Havana, Cuba, through the Panama Canal. The vessel made its way up the west coast of North America and moored in San Francisco, California.

Under palm trees and the hot California sun, Peter was introduced to formal art training and the glitzy world of Hollywood. To help pay his school fees, he worked as a chauffeur, driving movie stars and film industry bigwigs. A likeable fellow who told compelling stories, Peter was also an attentive listener who befriended many of the people he drove. He had a subtle charm that drew others to him.

In 1924 after a year in California, Peter returned to Banff. He found several artists had arrived in Banff. Acting as an apprentice, Peter honed his skills with the help of such masters as Carl Rungius, J. E. H. MacDonald, and New England artist Aldro T. Hibbard. Peter accompanied Carl Rungius in the field when Carl stayed in Banff. Carl had built a studio home in Banff in 1921 named "The Paintbox," where he stayed from April to October of each year. His anatomically accurate big game paintings and muted, textured landscape paintings made an impression on Peter. J. E. H. MacDonald began making annual trips to the Lake O'Hara region beginning the autumn of 1924. Peter was captivated by MacDonald's ability to capture the essence of the scenery and the vibrant yellow larches that filled the valley. He accompanied MacDonald to ease the visitor's fears of the wilderness and wild animals, and grew to enjoy MacDonald's company.

Peter continued to learn new techniques. In 1925, he painted alongside Aldro T. Hibbard at Lake O'Hara. Aldro encouraged Peter to consider studying at his alma mater, the School of the Museum of Fine Arts in Boston. Peter's decision to study at this eastern school affected the course of his life profoundly. Yet Aldro's most important connection to the Whytes was yet to come.

# Chapter 3
# Romance Blossoms

*"Before I had you everything seemed rather empty,*
*but now I feel as though life really held something for*
*me after all. I knew ever so long ago that I would find*
*you somewhere, long before I ever went to Boston, but*
*I wondered where and when. Now that I have you I*
*couldn't ever bear to part with you."*
Letter from Peter to Catharine May 15, 1928

A mong the pieces of art that compete for visitors' attention at the Whytes' home in Banff is a large canvas depicting the enormous face of Mount Biddle, a prominent mountain of the Lake O'Hara region. Catharine fell in love with this painting when she toured Aldro T. Hibbard's studio with some art school chums in 1926. Among the students was a dark-haired boy from Canada whom she found amusing. He knew the area depicted in Aldro's painting well. Little did Catharine know, but in a few short years she would slip into the scene the artist had created. She would smell the sweetness of the yellow larch. She would breathe in the crisp alpine air. She would become acquainted with the grandness of the mountains.

Peter knew Catharine belonged in Aldro T. Hibbard's scene long before she did. The couple met in Boston at the School of the Museum of Fine Arts in 1925. In her journal Catharine described Peter as "a Scotch friend" after their first meeting. Peter, however, felt an instant connection. He knew from the beginning that Catharine was a special person he wanted to spend more time with. That same year he clipped a picture of Catharine dressed for the opera out a page from a society column in the newspaper. He kept that clipping his entire life. However, it took time, reams of romantic love letters, and finally, the giving up of an old flame, before Catharine succumbed to her feelings for Peter.

**Early Courtship**
Catharine initially enrolled as a part-time student at the School of the Museum of Fine Arts because she

was unsure whether art was her calling. She soon changed her status to full time because she enjoyed her classes so much.

The program at Boston's prestigious art school was quite traditional. Students were trained to draw realistic representations of what they saw. This approach suited both Peter and Catharine — neither cared for the modernist style. The two friends were considered talented students. Peter won scholarships for his art every year that he attended the school. These scholarships, along with the money he earned working, allowed him to continue his studies. Catharine was a skilled artist, especially in figure drawing. In her second year at school, Catharine won the Concours, an art school competition.

Catharine and Peter began to spend time together in 1926, attending art exhibitions and social functions with friends. Once, Peter took Catharine to see his friend Carl Rungius' work. Catharine admired Peter's dedication to art and his experience of working alongside famous artists.

Peter shared his love of the mountains with Catharine throughout their budding relationship. While Peter was in Banff during the summer of 1927, he bought a keepsake for Catharine. It was a hood ornament in the shape of a buffalo. Catharine was nonplussed by the gift, but she fastened it to the front of her Packard to spare Peter's feelings. Other gifts from Peter included a Hudson's Bay Company wool blanket and a native headdress. Peter felt the need to share his love of his home town with his closest friend at art school. In doing so, he was opening up his heart to Catharine.

Peter wrote frequently to Catharine when he was away from Boston. In order to earn enough money to cover living expenses and tuition for art school, Peter had to leave school early each semester and resume his work for the Brewster Transport Company in Banff. Since this left only six months of the year for studying, Peter condensed his training in Boston by going to school six days a week and taking supplemental night classes at the Massachusetts Normal Art School.

In December 1927, Peter wrote Catharine a letter while travelling across Alberta by train working as a security guard. It was –46 degrees Celsius in the rail car, but nevertheless he took out his pen and paper to scratch a letter to Catharine. He wrote, "Kay, it seemed as though the Rockies were putting on a special day for me because I have never seen them with such wonderful colour, lights, shadows, and such pure-looking snow. They are real friends. I wish, Kay, that you could know them." Their relationship had deepened and Peter's correspondence had become more intimate. His letters were longer and more frequent, averaging more than 10 pages a week.

Catharine confided in her journal, "The girls think I am crazy to go with him so much. They don't find him interesting and think he's conceited if he talks about what he's interested in. I'm beginning to find Peter a real person and a wonderful friend." Catharine's girlfriends did not understand him at all. They were accustomed to talking about parties, fashion, and the latest gossip. Peter's stories about ski jumping, hiking, and the mountains made their eyes glaze over.

In Peter's eyes, Catharine stood out from all the other girls. He instinctively knew she had a kind heart and open mind. She was interested in learning about far away places and discussing topics other than her social calendar. Peter was not one for "polite" conversation. He would rather be alone than with someone whose company he didn't particularly enjoy. Peter was honest and straightforward, even when communicating his feelings for Catharine: "I don't like flattering people and I know you resent such things and I do also, but when I say something about you Kay, I mean it, and although I sometimes do not express myself clearly, still I know we understand each other."

When Catharine's father died in February 1927, she turned to Peter for comfort. Catharine had loved her father dearly and his death was hard on her. Peter was a good listener and was a pillar of support while she was grieving. The trauma brought the pair closer together.

Despite the lack of approval from her friends, Peter and Catharine continued to flirt and spend time together. They made a bet with each other: because Catharine had such a strong belief in Peter's artistic ability, she bet him that he would become a famous artist. He bet against this projection. It was decided that the winner of the bet would take the loser on a painting trip somewhere remote, such as Herschel Island in the Arctic, where they could paint an unfamiliar landscape.

From the beginning of their relationship, travel was an enthusiastic topic of conversation. The two friends spent hours dreaming of faraway places, planning imaginary trips and adventures. Both Catharine and Peter were already well travelled when they met. Catharine had visited many places in the United States and Canada — including Banff when she was younger. After high school, before her debutante year, she had journeyed around Europe for four months with her family. Meanwhile, Peter had explored much of Canada and the United States by train, and had also sailed through the Panama Canal. He was planning a trip to Asia after he completed art school. Their common desire to see more of the world cemented their relationship.

**Caught Up in Love**

Peter's feelings for Catharine were openly reciprocated in the spring of 1928. Catharine confided in her journal how much she cared for Peter and how she enjoyed his company. She wrote "we can discuss the deepest subjects in the oddest places, at a hockey game, or in a noisy restaurant." The couple frequented a restaurant called Cerulean Blue, a cosy spot located halfway between their apartments in Boston. Here they would sit for hours discussing "everything from Religion to Art to Skiing," enjoying a good meal, and revelling in each other's company.

One evening while playing bridge with the girls, Catharine abruptly left the game and ran to the train station to see Peter off. He was on his way to Lake Placid for a ski-jumping competition. She explained her erratic behaviour in her journal, "I thought of Peter's train stopping at eight. So I dashed for the station, arriving as it came in. As the train started up, I spied Peter looking out the window and I had time to shout, 'Good Luck' and he was gone." This show of affection meant a great deal to Peter, who wrote to her from the train, "Usually when we go to a tournament we ski for someone, and this time I am skiing for Catharine Robb!"

When Peter returned from Lake Placid, his budding relationship with Catharine blossomed. The two were inseparable. They talked for hours, dreaming about their future. They were caught up in the exhilaration of being with someone who is enjoying your company as much as you are enjoying theirs. The couple shared their most private hopes, dreams, and desires with each other. They explored their philosophies on life and religion, and their desire to lead a creative, helpful life.

Catharine's journal entries became a little muddled around this period. She did not write for long stretches of time and when she did, her entries were buoyant, fragmented exclamations about dreamy days spent with her beau. Her usually well-ordered description of events was lost in a quick scrawl of feelings. She gushed, "Things were happening so thick and fast that days meant nothing to me ... we never missed an opportunity to be together."

Any woman's heart would melt after reading

Peter's letters to Catharine. On April 9, 1928, he wrote "This is the longest letter I have ever written and have never enjoyed writing so before in my life. You have most certainly wakened me up and made me realize I am alive, and now I see ever so much more pleasure in doing things. Everything I do from now on will be done with thoughts of you and the most important things are to be done for you. There isn't anything I wouldn't do for you, Catharine."

## A Secret Affair

Catharine and Peter kept their relationship a secret for more than two years. Peter understood Catharine's wish to keep their relationship quiet. Catharine couldn't bear to be the centre of attention or to have people gossip about her. Peter understood this. He wrote, "You did what was right Kay in not mentioning me to anyone because I understand the embarrassing position it would put you in. I respect you too much to place you where you wouldn't want to be. What the rest of the students do not know will not hurt them."

The couple went to elaborate lengths to disguise the depth of their relationship. They wrote in tiny handwriting so their letters would not bulge and divulge a fondness for each other that was beyond friendly correspondence. They sent letters only once a week so the frequency of their correspondence would not arouse suspicion. However, as the relationship progressed, they both found it hard to limit what they wanted to say and how often they wanted to say it.

Unable to contain his writing, Peter asked Catharine if he could send his letters to both her school and her home. This way, her family and friends would only know about half the letters they sent each other. They even wrote decoy letters that could be shared with family. Their "real" letters were kept private. Peter explained to Catharine, "Enclosed you will find the letter which you can show to the girls and later I will write one which you can show to your family. It sounds rather cold-blooded, but will be enough for anyone else to see. Let anyone think or say what they may, I am all yours and love you above everything." Throughout the school year, the couple avoided each other in public settings, preferring secret meetings. This escapade was thrilling at first, but the appeal began to wane.

Catharine began to fear that their charade, though initially exciting, would only be hurtful in the end. As the couple became more serious and talked of marriage, she reconsidered their relationship's clandestine nature. In 1929, Catharine and two friends travelled to Banff to visit Peter. The trip offered Catharine an opportunity to inspect what would become her new home. In Banff, she met Peter's friends and family, and explored the captivating landscape. The two even travelled alone together for a short time. Catharine's family still did not know the extent of their relationship.

The secretive nature of their relationship became overwhelming for Catharine — she needed a confidante. Although Catharine and Peter had been planning to meet secretly in England later that year, Catharine felt that she should finally tell her family the truth. Her secret was disclosed in the autumn of 1929. While staying with family in Gorham, Massachusetts, she told her favourite aunt Nela. Lying in bed together one night, Catharine revealed to her aunt the details of her relationship with a young man she met at art school. She explained how Peter's views about the world meshed so well with her own and how much the two of them cared for each other. Aunt Nela was happy that Catharine had found someone who made her feel this way and urged her to tell the rest of the family.

When she returned home from Gorham, Catharine told her mother that she was planning to get married and asked her to guess the identity of her fiancé. Edith Morse Robb guessed correctly. To Catharine's surprise, her mother was pleased about the engagement. Feeling braver, Catharine told her brother, again making him guess who her husband would be. After guessing incorrectly a couple of times, Russell finally got the suitor's name right. He, too, was delighted for his sister. It was nanny Jean who was disappointed. She was concerned that Catharine would be giving up a life of privilege and the possibility of doing important charitable work. Indeed, the whole family worried about how Catharine would adapt to living so far away from home. However, the anticipation of a wedding thrilled Edith Morse Robb. Soon, the planning consumed her. Any concerns about the marriage itself were blanketed by guest lists, wedding gown shopping, preparing the home, and anticipating the big day.

**A Tough Decision**
During the months before the wedding, lingering doubts mingled with her excitement. Catharine was torn between the comfortable, conventional life she knew and a life as a free-spirited artist with exotic travel and uncharted possibilities. She contemplated

her choices in her diary: "We could be painting in China and seeing life. I wouldn't look forward with as much anticipation if I thought I were to lead a conventional existence 'round Boston, even with Maine in the summer, and yet, Buz, it takes a good deal of courage to think of China." She realized the incredible change that would occur in her life. It was both an exciting and terrifying prospect.

Catharine's last-minute jitters were expressed in letters to Peter because he was travelling again. Catharine still held a place in her heart for John D. Rockefeller III right up until months before her marriage to Peter. She wrote to Peter explaining her feelings for John: "I do believe I loved him awfully well as a young girl would, and I guess I'll always have some feeling left. I can't help it. If he hadn't hurt me so by not dancing with me and not paying any real attention to me, I probably would still be thinking myself a martyr, but my common sense told me I wasn't the proper person for him. He doesn't like to walk or look at beautiful places." Despite her openness about her feelings for John, Catharine assured Peter that she cared deeply for him: "You are worth millions of other people to me. You are just different, that's all, and I never have loved anyone in the way I do you."

During their engagement, between October

1929 and May 1930, Peter travelled to Japan, China, Hong Kong, Hawaii, Italy, and then back to the Orient. He financed his trip by selling several of his paintings for $50 each. He also worked for the Royal Hawaiian Transport Company and on steamships to fund his passage. Working and living conditions onboard were demanding. Crew members toiled through the night shovelling coal to keep the steamer moving, then were expected to be on deck the next day working in the equatorial sun's blistering heat. True to his mountain roots, Peter preferred to sleep in the open air on deck rather than down below in the stench of the crew quarters. For Peter the hard work was worth it because he enjoyed his time in port so much. Photographing and sketching lives so different from his own intrigued him.

The long-distance nature of Catharine and Peter's relationship prior to the wedding was a blessing in many ways. It gave them time to contemplate their hopes and dreams and share these sentiments via the thoughtful medium of the written word. Peter's consistent letter writing and soothing, measured feelings were reassuring to the nervous Catharine. Catharine wrote to Peter at the beginning of his trip, "Mother will not see how we can be so far away from each other and be in love because she never could be away from father a minute and she has an idea that the more you love a person the more you want to be with him. Well that is true but she doesn't realize the more you love a person the more willing you are to be separated."

Catharine's measured journal entries in the run up to the wedding display an increasing sense of peace with regards her decision to marry Peter. "With Peter I feel so independent and sure and unhurried. If he wants to spend more than a year on the trip he can and know I will understand. If I wanted to do the same, or something I couldn't do with him, he'd feel the same. When we are together we are working for something greater than ourselves. We must both give up a lot I suppose, but 'those who lose their life shall find it'. I never realized before that Peter had given up skiing to study Art, that he had really considered an athletic outdoor life. I might have gone on with a social life and a lot of charities."

Despite Catharine's relaxed attitude to time spent apart, Peter's return was greatly anticipated. Like a scene from a romance movie, the couple agreed to meet at the Savoy Hotel in London at noon. Catharine wrote, "I wonder who'll be there first. I bet I will. I love life and I love you and everything! It's going to be perfect going with you after noon at the

Savoy." Although they both knew that Peter's trip would be over in May, they did not know exactly which day they would meet up. The precise date was left to fate and the promise that they would wait for each other.

# Chapter 4
# En Plein Air

*"When I am to be married it will be in a large
church and in June, either when the peonies
are out or the larkspur and roses, one or the other,
and I shall have a reception outdoors, on the lawn,
and I and My Husband will stand on the
piazza or else under the apple tree ... "*
Catharine's journal entry June 24, 1922, age 17

On June 30, 1930, Peter Whyte and Catharine Robb were married under the apple tree in front of 300 guests on the Robb estate. Catharine's white dress had long, sheer sleeves and a cut that slid gracefully over her slender figure. Layers of tulle cascaded in fairy-like drapes to her ankles. She wore a billowy veil that trailed about a metre behind. Her wavy brown hair was swept off her face and secured in a loose bun at the nape of her neck. In photographs her new husband took of her, she has a broad smile. She looks joyously expectant of the adventure that awaits.

After the wedding, the couple packed as much as they could fit into Catharine's Packard. Only a fraction of the 400 or more gifts they received would fit in the car. Silver, vases, lamps, fine furniture, and kitchen supplies were loaded in trunks. These would be shipped later. Catharine left many familiar riches behind as she and her new husband sped away for a new life together.

The newlyweds spent a month driving cross-country, exploring New York, Wisconsin, Minnesota, and Montana. Along the way, they stayed with family and friends. Bumping along side roads and cruising down long stretches of highway, the couple had ample time to talk about their new life together. Instead of writing their thoughts, now they could communicate directly, sharing their hopes and dreams.

**A New Home**
They arrived in Banff in late August of 1930. The leaves were changing from apple green to vivid yellow. The people of Banff had been expecting

them, and were waiting to scrutinize Peter Whyte's new bride.

Catharine wrote home faithfully to her mother. Throughout their lives, Catharine and her mother always kept in close correspondence, writing to each other at least a few times a week. Edith Morse Robb lived to be 98 years old and she kept all of her daughter's letters. There are thousands of them, each one long and carefully written. In their correspondence, they shared what was happening in their lives, recommended good books, and shared their views on the state of world affairs.

Many of Catharine's early letters informed her mother about the people she met. It didn't take long for Catharine to become part of the town's social circle. At the time, there were few permanent residents in Banff. She wrote home after attending a tea hosted by the wife of the Banff Springs Hotel manager: "I wish you could have seen the funny combination of people, for society in Banff is quite small-townish. People like Mrs. Rungius and Mrs. Painter and people like that who go up to the hotel quite a bit and have lived in New York and other places, and then one or two who try to be socialites and doll up fit to kill. I was by far the youngest, by nearly 20 years I guess, but it was fun and I did enjoy it." Catharine's friendly personality allowed her to seamlessly slip into any social situation. Her society background had given her the skills to converse with just about anyone. She also had a genuine interest in what others did — a keen awareness that everyone had special qualities and interesting lives. Catharine fit in at ladies' luncheons, as a guest in homes on the Morley native reserve, hiking with groups of mountain men, and with her new family.

Peter and Catharine lived with Peter's mother and father while their home was being built. Dave and Annie White welcomed their new daughter-in-law. She was bright and kind, and proved to be a good match for their son. As a wedding present, Peter's parents gave the couple a plot of land. When the newlyweds designed their new home, they chose a log cabin with a large, open room to be used as a studio.

During construction, the newlyweds would often stop by to check on progress. The smell of cut lumber mixed with the fresh mountain air when they made late-night pilgrimages to the site. Their excitement grew. In May 1931, the new house was finished. Nestled between tall spruce trees on their grassy plot of land between the Bow River and downtown Banff, the Whytes' log home was rustic, but comfortable.

Peter and Catharine unpacked some of their

lavish wedding gifts, but quickly repacked much of the silver and fancy home furnishings because the items did not belong with the rest of the décor. John D. Rockefeller III had given the couple a Japanese ceramic lamp with a fine silk shade. Catharine adapted the lamp to the surroundings by crowning it with a shade she made from parchment and buckskin. Their home was welcoming with folksy touches and an eclectic mixture of styles.

The couple received a flood of visitors in the first few months after they moved in. Catharine recounts the frequency of callers to her mother, "We counted for the fun of it, how many different people had been in the house since the middle of May and there were over a hundred we could remember. Nearly all of them have to have tea or something." Peter and Catharine's home would become a popular stop for locals, Stoneys, and other visitors. Eventually, additions were made to their home and the art studio was moved upstairs allowing the artists to work uninterrupted.

**Art and Adventure**
Some of Peter and Catharine's most popular portraits were created in the 1930s. The two travelled to Morley to paint the striking features of their Stoney

friends. One of Peter's most famous paintings features Mrs. Tom Simeon. She is dressed in a vibrant red smock against a butter-yellow background. The portrait displays Peter's eye for colour. The painting was accepted by the jury of the National Academy of Design, and the American Federation of the Arts showed it in a travelling exhibition.

Catharine's portraits were also well received. She had an ability to capture the spirit of the people she painted. Although she preferred to withhold judgment about whose paintings were better, Catharine did admit that she favoured her own portrait of Tom Wilson over Peter's. In Catharine's painting, there is a twinkle in his eye and a familiar assurance in his gaze. Catharine was adept at capturing her subject's personality and reflecting it through her art.

Throughout the 1930s, Peter and Catharine received many visitors who came to have their portraits painted. The young couple used a little cabin on their property as a guesthouse for portrait subjects. It was also used by visiting Stoney friends so they would not have to make the journey home to the reserve in darkness.

During the first years of their marriage, Peter and Catharine spent a great deal of time touring the West. The couple financed their travels partially with money earned from sales of their artwork, but mainly through Catharine's trust fund. Theirs was a comfortable lifestyle that allowed them the freedom to pursue their dreams. Finally, Peter was able to show Catharine the mountain passes he had described in his letters. They set off almost every day to a new location, each one worthy of an artist's attention. The couple spent a lot of time scouting landscapes and searching for people they could paint portraits of. They travelled around Alberta, British Columbia, and the northwestern United States. They also extensively hiked the Rocky Mountains with friends and fellow painters.

They would often pack a picnic lunch for an all-day excursion on a remote trail, which they would ascend until they found a suitable place to sketch. Once the location was chosen, they would set up their easels close to one another and spend the entire day striving to capture the majesty of nature on canvas. Trained to paint in an interpretive yet realistic manner, the Whytes' sketches and oil paintings reflect the mountains, valleys, glaciers, trees, and rivers with the appreciation of people who truly celebrated their surroundings. The details of their paintings show the stratification of rock and the mutability of mountain weather and light. Deep browns and moody greys contrast with watery blues and energizing greens. The yellow larches of Lake O'Hara and Bow Lake, two of Catharine and Peter's favourite locations, appear vibrant under early autumn snow.

In the first years of their marriage, Peter took Catharine to all his favourite places. Trekking up steep, rocky trails in extreme temperatures was a far cry from the comfortable confines of a Boston living room, but Catharine thrived. She delighted in her new life. In photographs taken during this time, Catharine looks completely at home in rolled-up jeans and layers of sweaters, grinning for the camera.

It was during these early days that the photograph that would later be used as the logo for the Whyte Museum of the Canadian Rockies was taken. It was snapped at the summit of Abbot Pass above Lake Oesa. Catharine and Peter left Lake Louise at 5:30 in the morning to climb the steep ascent of Abbot Pass with a group of friends. The pass is notoriously dangerous. Hikers have to beware of falling rock and treacherous crevasses. In the photograph, Catharine is standing on top of a spire of rock with the party's Swiss guide, Rudolph Aemmer, standing on a ledge below. Peter is poised precariously below him, and fellow hiker Neil Begg stands at the bottom.

In her letters home, Catharine offered details of

her new life that must have made poor Mrs. Robb shudder. However, Catharine always wrote about her exciting adventures in a positive, and often humorous, way. She wrote, "I learnt quite a bit Sunday. One convenient thing to know is how to blow one's nose without a handkerchief, for noses run continually when it's as cold as it was. Something like 'The Night Before Christmas.' Remember the part 'and laying a finger aside of his nose, he gave me a nod, up the chimney he rose'? You do all except the rising up the chimney." Catharine was becoming a mountain woman.

# Chapter 5
# Running Skoki Lodge

**M**ountains frame the Skoki Valley near Lake Louise and coniferous trees dot the valley bottom. In winter, their boughs become heavy with soft piles of snow. The sun kisses the snowy carpet, turning each flake into a spark of shimmering light. Wisps of clouds glide by, mirroring the snow's fluffy surface. Skoki is a treed haven amid the jagged peaks, and is an area that was close to Catharine and Peter's hearts.

To get to Skoki Valley at that time, skiers had to traverse more than 22 kilometres through the

Ptarmigan Valley, over Boulder Pass, past Ptarmigan Lake, and up the aptly named Deception Pass. The long, steep climb of this second pass is countered by a descent that zips skiers into a skiing playground. Building a ski lodge in the middle of this winter wonderland was a dream realized by an ambitious group of young skiers that included Peter, Catharine, and their friends and family. Peter's older brother Cliff and his friend, Cyril Paris, originally had the idea to erect a cabin in the area. The idea was supported by the 50 or so members of the Ski Club of the Canadian Rockies.

In September 1930, the National Parks Bureau granted permission to build, and construction began immediately. The hardworking crew packed in supplies by foot and dogsled. In less than three months, they had built a large, log cabin to serve as the main lodge. In 1931, a kitchen was added to the back of the lodge, two dormitory cabins were built to serve as sleeping quarters for guests, and a second cabin — known affectionately as "Halfway Hut" — was built in the Ptarmigan Valley, halfway between the train station at Lake Louise and Skoki Lodge. When they were not travelling, Peter and Catharine helped with the construction, promotion, and preparation of the area for guests. Beginning in 1932, the young couple took

Skiers near Skoki, 1932

over the operation of Skoki, including the debts incurred during construction, from Cliff White, who was having financial difficulties. They agreed to run Skoki for five years, after which time Cliff would reimburse them and reclaim the lodge.

During the first few years she lived in Banff, Catharine spent most of her time in the company of

Peter's male friends. It was no different at Skoki. She wrote that this companionship suited her: "It's nice being the only lady in camp, as Peter and I have the ladies' cabin to ourselves." A strong woman who could hold her own, Catharine easily fit in with male company.

Despite being new to ski touring, Catharine was an exceptionally good sport about the difficulty of the Skoki journey. On one of the first missions to scout the area, Peter, Catharine, and some friends encountered near-blizzard conditions. Snow covered the unmarked trail and the crew was thrown off course. They veered miles from their destination and had to wade through hip-deep snow in a whiteout of pelting snow. Stopping to eat what was left of their meagre lunches, the group revaluated their course and, finally, neared their destination. Despite the party's protests, Catharine broke trail for parts of the epic trek.

Many supply trips would be made before the cabins at Skoki were completed. Catharine merrily reported their strenuous activities in letters to her mother: "There were eight men and two dog teams and between us we have managed to bring in over 3200 pounds of provisions, bedding and stoves etc. We packed in four stoves! Fourteen miles! Over two mountain passes!" Although Catharine was slender, she was strong — and a natural athlete. She appears in photographs dressed in layers of men's clothing, her hair tucked under a beret, exposing a tanned face and huge grin. Peter also looks energized, sporting checked shirts, wool pants, and suspenders, with his sleeves rolled up, ready to work.

Once the buildings were erected, the group focussed on maintaining the area. They spent a good portion of their day shovelling snow and preparing the lodges for guests. Even digging a path around the lodge and to the outhouse — what Catharine called the "Whoseitswhatsit" — was tiring. The snow that piled up along the banks after a walking path had been cleared would sometimes reach a man's shoulders. Metres of snow accumulated during a winter season. Other on-going jobs included preparing food for the hungry workers and guests, collecting water, and chopping wood to heat the cabins.

**Fun and Frolic**
Catharine and Peter didn't spend all their time working. The crews building and running Skoki Lodge made sure they compensated for their workload with a good dose of fun. This common goal strengthened their camaraderie. Practical jokes, snowball fights,

and plenty of days spent skiing kept spirits high. Friendly downhill races were waged. Sometimes, the goal was to be the most outlandishly dressed skier on the hill; other times, the goal was to beat the rest of the pack down the slopes.

Photographs taken from Skoki's early days reveal the happiness of the people who took part in building the dream. In many pictures, their arms are draped around one another in a show of comfortable affection. They look carefree in their existence away from civilization. They worked hard and played hard, sharing a communal table, work ethic, and passion for skiing.

Peter's photographs from this time feature friends making turns on the slopes, sailing into the air over steep jumps, and racing through the trees, their shoulders skimming branches. In many of Peter's photographs, the skiers stand like half-peeled bananas, bearing bathing suit tops or bare chests, jackets tied snugly at their waists. They lean happily against their ski poles for a quick snap of the camera and a short rest before hitting the slopes again.

Peter also created playful, colourful cartoons of their adventures in the backcountry. Some portray groups of skiers whizzing down slopes; others feature friends leaping through the air, with knees bent and feet tucked as though they are about to cannonball into a pool. He captured the occasional fallen comrade — skis and poles sticking out of mounds of snow like porcupine quills, the skier a laughing heap, limbs akimbo.

Niall and Lady Jean Rankin from England were among the lodge's first international guests. The couple enjoyed their stay so much they helped publicize Skoki through glowing written reports of their adventures in various British journals. The visitors also donated a silver cup that served as the prize for an annual ski race down Pika Peak — the Rankins' favourite slope. Before long, guests from all over the world began trickling in. Catharine's connections in the eastern United States also helped to lure some of Skoki's early guests. Catharine's brother, Russell Robb, came from Boston for a couple of weeks to ski and catch up with his sister in the spring of 1932. Tourists arrived in different degrees of preparedness. Some came lacking proper outdoor attire and equipment. Their hosts remedied such situations by loaning out ski boots, skis, and even mittens.

Peter and Catharine enjoyed the company of their enthusiastic guests. Catharine draped warm blankets over the lodge's furniture and hung paintings on the walls to make the atmosphere homey. The fireplace crackled in the evenings as guests and staff played cards and swapped stories. Catharine wrote home relaying some of the guests' most interesting tales, describing the enjoyment she gained from these relaxing evenings.

## Tragedy Strikes

In 1933, a dark shadow was cast over Skoki's light-hearted atmosphere. Dr. Raymond Edwin Allen Christopher Paley, was a brilliant mathematician who had recently been appointed to the Massachusetts Institute of Technology on a Rockefeller scholarship. He was part of a group of Bostonians who came to Skoki in early spring. Paley was a bit of a loner, and he preferred to ski on his own. His solitary wanderings worried the others. Catharine wrote, "The day we went to the Grindelwald he dashed off alone before anyone knew where he was headed and we suddenly saw him climbing the most dangerous slope you can imagine. Luckily he got back down safely and everyone lit into him about doing such a foolhardy thing." The next time that Paley ventured out on his own he was not as lucky.

After lunch on April 7, without the knowledge of the group, Paley left the lodge and made a beeline for the steep slopes of nearby Fossil Mountain — an area that had recently been deemed unsafe by more experienced skiers. The sky was heavy and grey as he neared the summit of the 2900-metre mountain. Suddenly, violent gusts of wind whipped around the top of the mountain creating a whiteout of blinding snow. Slippery patches of ice interspersed patches of crusty snow. A short distance from the summit, Paley's skis skidded. His 100-kilogram mass triggered the release of huge slabs of snow. The force of the slide sent Paley over a cliff in an avalanche of snow and rock.

Peter and a member of the tour group had set off to pick up supplies at Halfway Hut early that afternoon. They noticed Paley's solitary tracks ahead of them and followed them to the base of the avalanche site. They could see no tracks leading out, so they began frantically searching for him. The howling winds, cold temperatures, failing light, and threat of another slide stopped their search before the body was uncovered. Early the next morning, searchers began the dismal task again. When they found Paley's body, they brought it to Lake Louise for authorities to examine. Peter, as the head guide, bore the brunt of the authorities' interrogation.

The accident shook everyone at Skoki. Catharine wrote to her mother with news of the catastrophe:

"You will have received the wire we sent in case the paper made too much of the story. It really was a most unfortunate accident, but though we tried to stop Paley from going off alone he would insist on doing it and unfortunately went off a slope that avalanched during a change in temperature yesterday. There is never any need for us to go off alone on any questionable slope. It isn't as if we hadn't warned Paley, for every one of us had."

Paley's mother, who lived in London, wrote to Peter and Catharine searching for more information about her son's death. After hearing the full story, she began to come to terms with her son's passing. Some time later, she claimed to have spoken to her son through a medium. His spirit told her about the veils of snow that whipped around the peak, the cracking snow beneath his feet, and the fall that broke his neck and knees. Paley's mother believed that he must have been working out a mathematical problem while skiing alone and was not thinking clearly about the danger he faced.

The Rockefeller Foundation sent an investigator to question Peter about the accident. Rehashing the events weighed heavily on him. The mere suggestion of guilt was hard for him to bear. After a three-day interrogation, the Rockefeller Foundation's final report stated that: "all the blame of the accident must rest on Mr. Paley himself." Even though he was in no way responsible, Peter felt terrible about the accident. Catharine explained the couple, "couldn't seem to get the thing out of our minds." It would haunt Peter for the rest of his life. The accident cast a blanket of darkness on the rest of the season. Despite attempts to carry on, the couple found they were too affected by the tragedy to return to the same level of enjoyment they once felt. As soon as they were able, Peter and Catharine closed Skoki for the year. Jim Boyce, who had been a cook and outfitter at Skoki, took over its operations for the remainder of the Whytes' five-year agreement. Peter and Catharine embarked on a world trip that would keep them away from the painful memories.

# Chapter 6
# Faraway Lands

I n the fall of 1933, the couple visited Catharine's mother in Concord, then boarded a cross-country train that took them from Chicago to San Francisco. From the west coast, they boarded a steamer that would transport them across the Pacific Ocean to the island paradise of Hawaii. For a few months, they stayed in a bungalow on the beach of Hanalei Bay, Kauai. Catharine wrote to her mother that Kauai was, "without a doubt ... the loveliest place you ever saw." They enjoyed Hawaii's pleasant climate and rich culture.

Throughout their lives, Catharine and Peter would remain interested in Hawaiian folklore, dance, and musical traditions. For years they religiously recorded a radio broadcast of Hawaiian music called "Hawaii Calls" from the comfort of their Banff living room.

The couple were entranced by the orange-pink glow of the sun as it descended into the sea each evening. They were equally enthralled watching the rising of the moon as it cast white beams that reflected off the lapping waves. Peter and Catharine's art collection contains numerous sketches of the Hawaiian landscape. They also painted oil portraits of the Hawaiian locals they befriended.

Early in 1934, Peter and Catharine were excited to discover they could buy round the world tickets at a special couples rate of only $537 each, a discount of $226. The refundable tickets were valid for two years, allowed them to book their passage as they travelled, and permitted them to stay wherever they wanted for as long as they wanted. The deal couldn't be better! They wrote home to let everyone know they were leaving Honolulu on a journey around the world.

Their first stop was Japan. Catharine wrote to her mother, requesting her grandfather's book about his travels in Japan called *Japan Day by Day*. The couple wanted to get a sense of his perspective before they explored the country on their own. They also arranged to visit some of her grandfather's old pupils and friends. Catharine was in awe of her new surroundings. She wrote a detailed travelogue to her mother about the "tiny streets, gray wooden houses, bits of gardens, washing hanging on bamboo poles instead of lines, flower pots with tiny trees on windowsills, little babies being lugged about on people's backs, other children like bright balls wrapped in so much clothing. Bicycles everywhere, people carrying every kind of thing on either end of a pole balanced on the shoulder. Men and women hoeing in gardens with the kind of hoe Grandpa described. It is all so interesting and hard to believe."

During their travels, Peter took many photographs. The couple also sketched and painted as much as time would allow. In Tokyo, they took lessons in Japanese brushwork from a man named Mr. Hotta. During their lessons, a young boy served as translator by looking up words in a dictionary. Still, the three artists were able to communicate well enough through their art. Mr. Hotta had the couple sign some of their paintings for him. The teacher thought Peter was particularly skilled at painting bamboo and Catharine at painting orchids. Peter and

Catharine spent six weeks in Japan painting, visiting, and touring the sights Catharine's grandfather had known so intimately.

From Japan, they took a passenger boat to China. They marvelled in the sights of Peking, Shanghai, and Hong Kong, and visited the Great Wall of China. Painting was more difficult in China. Every time they set up to sketch outdoors, they drew a crowd of onlookers peering over their shoulders. This rattled Catharine enough that she stopped sketching, while Peter focussed on his photography. After four weeks in China, they sailed to Bali and Java.

Here, Catharine was amazed by the brilliant magenta, scarlet, and ochre sarongs worn by the locals. She said, "it was like picking all shades of zinnias and combining them." The striking beauty of the locals inspired both artists to paint a number of portraits. As they did with landscapes, the couple would often paint the same person at the same time. Their portraiture bears similarities as they captured the same informal and unhurried lifestyle of the residents. Catharine and Peter painted the impish faces of young boys and the pretty profiles of young girls, patterned batik cloth tied around their heads.

After Bali and Java, a 17-day boat trip took the couple from Sumatra to Marseilles, France. Peter had never been to Paris before, so they headed north and toured the city's grand art museums and lounged in its cafés. In England, they trekked the cultured streets of London, soaked in the drunken, festive atmosphere of Germany during Oktoberfest, and hiked in the Swiss Alps. They would return to the Alps many times over the next 20 years. After 18 months away from family and friends, the couple returned to North America in the fall of 1934.

**A Lifetime of Travel**

From the beginning of Peter and Catharine's relationship, the thought of travelling together brought them closer. Both had the itch to visit faraway places: to take in the sights, sounds, smells, and experiences the world had to offer. Travel served as inspiration and fodder for their creative minds.

Their first trip together had been to Nassau in the West Indies. Shortly after they were married, in November 1931, the couple stopped in New York before sailing to Nassau in the Bahamas. Both Peter and Catharine had visited the Big Apple before, but exploring the city together was like seeing the city anew. For a day, they delighted in the hustle of the city, but they were equally excited to board the steamship to their destination that night.

A warm Caribbean breeze, pear trees, lush ferns, and roses in bloom greeted the couple in Nassau. They stayed in a large, sparsely decorated room with rough plaster walls that had been brushed over with a pastel green wash. Curtains fluttered softly in the breeze, keeping the room temperature pleasant despite the heat outside. Peter and Catharine revelled in the island's easygoing attitude. They lounged, read, and ate good food. Breakfast consisted of grapefruit, melons, pears, bananas, fish, eggs, and toast with guava jam. Days were spent leisurely sketching, swimming, sailing, and visiting with other guests. They spent the Christmas of 1931 in Jamaica. Island life suited the pair, and they would return to the West Indies and Hawaii throughout their lives.

In 1938, they embarked on a trip to Switzerland, Norway, and Scotland. The trip was cut short because of the tumultuous state of affairs in Europe. Peter wrote in September that he "didn't know what the world was coming to ... with the threat of war in Europe, a hurricane in New England, and continued good weather in Banff." The couple returned home just before the outbreak of the World War II.

## Chapter 7
# Official War Artist

orld War I had left an indelible imprint on Peter and Catharine's generation. Soldiers returning from the war were heroes and parties were thrown for them. Soldier worship infiltrated Catharine's young mind between the ages of 9 and 12, when World War I was raging. She fantasized that she was in the French army, and in her dream world she was part of a victory parade. Her lapel was heavy with medals and everyone was cheering for her. Catharine was too young to understand the horrors of war. Her

parents shielded her from the stories of death and destruction.

Peter was more aware of war's realities. In his junior high gym class, boys were taught how to shoot and shown how to use a bayonet. If the war had continued, Peter might have become a soldier in World War I. There were many enlistees from Banff. Becoming a soldier was a duty many young men were prepared for. When World War II loomed, Peter enlisted in the reserve army without hesitation.

In the summer of 1940, Peter took two weeks basic training with the Calgary Highlanders at the army's Sarcee camp. Boot camp was a challenge for a 35-year-old man who was accustomed to a comfortable life. His mountain skills and strong physique were valuable assets.

At the beginning of the war, the reserve army was not called upon, so after his training, Peter was sent home. But he wanted to be involved. He was too old to train as a pilot or aircrew, so he applied to join the air force as a photographer. In 1941, military administration told him that they would not be enlisting photographers for another month or two. So he spent the summer on an officer's training course offered by the reserve army. Peter served as quartermaster for the drill hall. His role was to ensure everything was working efficiently. Finally, in March 1943, he received a letter offering him a chance to enlist in the Royal Canadian Air Force in the skilled trades division as a photographer. He was sent to Edmonton for training and to take photographs. As a photographer for the air force, Peter took ID photos of soldiers, worked in the contact printing room, and even snapped wedding photos.

Peter missed Catharine, and, as in the years before their marriage, the couple relied on letter writing. Catharine filled Peter in with news from Banff and Peter replied with tales of daily operations at the camp. During the war, correspondence was closely monitored and even Catharine's letters home were censored. It was hard for them to be apart. Peter's first posting was in Vancouver. As soon as she could, Catharine moved to the west coast to live with him. Military life was full of impermanence, and in six short months, Peter was shuffled around six times. The couple had to be ready to pack up and move to another base with a couple of days notice. Peter was stationed back and forth between Vancouver, Patricia Bay near Victoria, and Tofino on Vancouver Island. The longest posting lasted several months in Tofino. Despite the lack of a permanent base, the couple enjoyed the atmosphere of the west coast and found time to sketch.

Everyone was affected by the war. In Banff, tourism slowed, as travelling away from home seemed both risky and frivolous. Gasoline rationing halted bus tours, and household rationing affected budgets. Catharine's brother left his high-paying, high-status job in Boston to enlist in the army. The Robbs donated thousands of dollars to the war effort and the Red Cross. Catharine became a member of the Red Cross and helped send packages to soldiers serving overseas.

Peter had joined the military with the hope of becoming a war artist and painting battle scenes overseas. In April 1944, he entered an oil sketch in an army art contest. His painting won second place. Along with the $50 prize money, Peter's painting attracted the attention of the military administration in Ottawa. He was made an official war artist. The Group of Seven painter A. Y. Jackson was on the committee that selected the war artists. He admired Peter's work and campaigned for his appointment. Jackson had served in World War I and had been an official war artist himself.

Peter was summoned to Ottawa for training. Being a war artist entitled him to more autonomy than most military personnel. He was allowed to move freely from station to station to capture military life on canvas. For three months, the war artists toured around Canadian bases with the promise of eventually being posted overseas, something that Peter had been hoping would happen for three years. Peter spent his term as official war artist in the Prairies. First, he stayed with soldiers at the Currie Barracks in Calgary painting airplanes and war machinery. After this stint, he moved to Fort McLeod, where Catharine joined him. As they had done in the mountains, Catharine and Peter would collect their painting materials and set off into the grassy fields until they found an ideal location. Each landscape presented its own challenges. In the mountains, light changes quickly; in the prairies, wind can be a tyrant. Peter solved the problem by attaching his painting supplies to a fence post. The couple quickly fell back into their routine of working a few metres away from each other and attempting to capture their surroundings. Catharine had trouble at first adjusting to the open prairie's brilliant light. It took a while for her eyes to adjust from gazing at the sun-blazed scenery to the easel.

The art world was flourishing during this period. Catharine contemplated the upsurge in artists' productivity during the war. She wrote to her mother,

"I wonder if the great destruction going on in the world has unconsciously made people want to create things." As adults, Catharine and Peter saw more clearly the horrors of war. Media broadcasts and newsreels brought the destruction and fear closer to home. Their romanticized notion of wartime dissipated as more and more soldiers lost their lives, entire cities were destroyed, and millions of civilians were killed.

For a couple of weeks in the fall of 1944, it appeared as though Peter might be sent overseas. However, by that time the air force was cutting back on expenditure and decided against sending him. Peter applied for a discharge on November 10, 1944. By January 1945, he was discharged and was able to resume painting freely. While serving as a war artist, he had created more than 50 paintings for war records.

Peter's Stoney friends were relieved to hear that he was no longer in the military. Walking Buffalo George McLean told Peter he overheard Mrs. McLean name Peter in her prayers. She "felt good in her heart" to know Peter was back to civilian life, safe and sound. War was over.

# Chapter 8
# Drawing Closer to Home

Art continued to be the Whytes' focus when they returned home to Banff after the war. Peter had experienced a taste of national recognition as an official war artist and it seemed that his artistic career was primed to take off. However, the post-war years ushered in a new phase of life for both Peter and Catharine. This was a period of challenges and difficulties for the couple. A battle with alcoholism, a lack of self-confidence, and cataracts took their toll on Peter's physical and mental health. Catharine wrestled with her desire to help her husband through these difficulties and her own needs as an artist. For the two decades following the end of World War II, the couple travelled less frequently.

Although the post-war period was not a prolific time for the Whytes, their art was celebrated. In 1947, George and Kathleen Pepper, artists and friends of the Whytes, brought their friend Clair Bice, Curator of the Public Library and Art Museum in London, Ontario, to Banff. She was delighted with Peter and Catharine's work, and the details for a travelling exhibition were hammered out. Nineteen paintings by Peter and sixteen of Catharine's were part of an exhibition that wowed crowds in Ontario towns including London, Windsor, Tilsonburg, Kitchener, Brantford, and Toronto, as well as in the eastern United States. The Peppers were able to attend some of the gallery openings and reported back to the couple that one opening night in particular was a "howling success that afforded us all a whole-wide-West full of pleasure." Eastern crowds enjoyed this close-up view of the legendary Rocky Mountains. Catharine and Peter were overjoyed at the level of interest in their work.

Long appreciated by talented visiting artists, some locals began to see the value of their friendly neighbours' work. Peter was asked to teach a couple of budding local artists. Two of his most committed students were the young Reverend of Banff, Mr. Tom Lonsdale, and a Stoney man from Morley named Frank Kaquitts. Peter taught the two men for free. He was a patient and kind teacher. Both students eventually won scholarships to the Banff School of Fine Arts (now The Banff Centre). Peter also encouraged watercolour artist Walter J. Phillips, who taught at the Banff School of Fine Arts for 20 years.

Despite their growing fame, Catharine and Peter's work did not receive the kind of national acclaim many people thought it merited. Some people believed this was because the Whytes did not actively pursue a course of self-promotion. Others artists, such as Group of Seven artist Lawren Harris, felt their location was an issue. He was also frank in his observations of Peter's alcoholism. He wrote to Catharine, imploring that the couple leave Banff and make a new start. He said, "There must be a new creative venture in art, a new life — and there must be a cure from alcoholism."

**Slowing Down**

Beginning in the late 1940s, Peter's emotional and physical health deteriorated. He became a very different person from the rugged mountain man he had once been. He grew reluctant to leave home. His adventurous spirit dissipated and he was preoccupied with worry. The seriousness of Peter's condition would wax and wane in the years before his death. Catharine reasoned that "worry is bound to tell on a person some way, and perhaps if you are sensitive enough to be an artist you take things differently than a businessman would." They were not completely housebound. They bought a jeep in 1946 that they used for occasional sketching excursions. They also bought a camper for short jaunts around western Canada and the United States, and they continued to make annual trips to Concord to visit Catharine's mother. When Peter felt well, they visited Hawaii and Europe.

Of her life during the 1950s and 1960s, Catharine wrote: "I have decided that life is a balancing of things. If you want one thing you have to give up another, you just can't have or do all you want, and it means trying to figure out which of the alternatives to choose. Peter and I have our life into the kind where we work as a team and we do practically everything together. We like it that way and feel we do better doing things together." Catharine was loyal to her husband and cared for him even when times were tough.

In many ways, Catharine led a very independent life compared to many women of her generation, but she shared the traditional belief that a woman's most important role was to support her husband. In 1953, she declared her occupation as "housewife" on her passport. In reality, along with her work as an artist, she did the bookkeeping, cleaned the house, and managed the couple's social obligations. Unfortunately, Catharine did not complete another large canvas after 1939 — she was too busy looking after household affairs and caring for Peter. She devoted more of her time to Banff community events, writing letters, and entertaining visitors.

**A Welcoming Home**
The Whyte home was an inviting place for visitors. Art covered the walls; everything from large canvases of mountain scenes, to West Coast native art and woodcarvings from the Pacific Islands. Japanese vases, hanging bronzes, and native drums were placed side-by-side. Several sets of miniature statues from around the world were lined up around the kitchen table, and hundreds of books were crammed into numerous bookshelves. A bronze statue of a horse sat on the mantelpiece close to a colourful painting depicting a native camp. Eighteen intricate-

ly beaded native belts hung from the stair railing. Mongolian stirrups were slung over a travelling trunk from the nineteenth century. An Indonesian batik table runner covered the solid oak table in the centre of the large living room. Floral embroidered footstools made by Catharine's mother rested near comfortable chairs in front of the fireplace. Stones, tree branches, gnarled pieces of wood, and other found objects nestled in nooks and crannies. Wafting out of the darkroom came the acidic aroma of developing tonic; the chalky smell of paint lingered in the air from the upstairs studio.

Peter and Catharine's home was a place where friends of all ages from around the world could come and hear a good story and, in turn, be listened to. Like the literary salons of Paris, the Whytes' eclectic log home served as the hub of Banff's cultural life. Artists of all sorts would convene here, including members of the Group of Seven, international visionaries, and local artisans. All were drawn to the home's eclectic style, artistic ambiance, and interesting inhabitants. Everyone, from the highest official to the 10-year-old paperboy called the two "Pete" and "Catharine." Tea was consumed in large quantities, and impromptu dinners were a regular occurrence. Humour was the dialect of the day and story swapping was the standard. Peter and Catharine strongly felt that the history of the Rocky Mountain region needed to be documented. They set about gathering people to record their tales on tape. Stoneys, local guides, climbers, and anyone who had an interesting story to tell had a forum for their remembrances at Peter and Catharine's home.

Many of the town's youths called on the couple. Troops of youngsters, including their many nieces and nephews, flooded their house after school for ginger ale and cookies. The children put on plays for Peter and Catharine, explored the house's treasures, and borrowed books. They were enthralled with these attentive, caring adults. Since Peter and Catharine did not have children of their own, they cherished these energizing visitors.

**Keeping in Touch**
The Whytes had made friends all over the world. Corresponding with everyone kept Catharine busy. Her letters were not whipped off in haphazard haste. They were long, well-constructed and well-written accounts of everyday events, feelings about current affairs, and ideas about the future. Her nephew Jon Whyte writes about Catharine's gifted correspondence in his book *Mountain Glory*: "People unfamil-

iar with the richness, variety and depth of Catharine's correspondence may not understand how much she invested her artistic expression in her letters." She ensured every encounter she had with people, be it by letter or in person, was a meaningful one.

Every December, Peter and Catharine faithfully sent out a Christmas card and letter to all their friends and family. Their greeting card list included hundreds of names — enough to fill 20 single-spaced pages. Each person received a long letter detailing what had happened to the couple that year. There were so many letters to print that they used the press at the *Banff Crag and Canyon*, the town's local newspaper. The card featured a sketch by Peter, which he and Catharine hand painted. In their Christmas letter of 1965, the Whytes shared the warm, generous spirit that made their home such a welcoming place: "We have enjoyed seeing old and new friends from near and far places and are always interested in their many endeavours. If by our encouragement we can increase their activities and accomplishments then we feel that indirectly we have done something worthwhile."

## Benefactors

The Whytes used their talents and resources to help others. They worked hard on their own projects, but also cared deeply about helping others accomplish their goals. They were fortunate to have the means to be able to live a comfortable life, but the couple lived modestly. Much of their money was donated to worthy causes and to help others realize their dreams.

Throughout their marriage, the couple helped finance family business endeavours, supplied numerous personal loans, and backed many community projects. They donated cash prizes for Banff Indian Days and spent time helping to organize the event. They gave regularly to charities such as the Red Cross, United Way, and the Unitarian Service Committee of Canada. They strongly supported medical research and local outdoors clubs. The couple also supported schools, clubs, and museums by donating money to places such as Harvard, Wheeler School, the Margaret Greenham School, and the Peabody Museum. This money was often given anonymously.

The couple did not just sign cheques. They provided support to many by listening, observing, and encouraging. One night their old friend Ike Mills came to Peter and Catharine's back door, tears of gratitude streaming down his face. He thanked them profusely for the package of food and dry goods they had set on his doorstep, knowing that he and his wife were going through some financial difficulties.

One vision that was close to their hearts was to provide a place where the culture, history, and stories of the Rocky Mountains could be preserved. They wanted others to share in the rich heritage and beauty of the Bow Valley that had been their home for so long. In their wills, they made provisions for the building of such a place.

## An Artist's Nightmare

In 1952, Peter found out that he had cataracts in both eyes. One eye was so affected that he had to have an operation right away. The procedure corrected his vision for a few years, but he lived in constant fear that the cataract in the other eye would worsen and he would lose his vision entirely. Six years after the first operation, Peter required surgery on his other eye. For a period between the operations he was blind in one eye, and though it was a struggle, he continued to paint. Overcoming this disability took courage and determination. During this period, Peter painted furiously in anticipation of the worst. Art patron Eric Harvie commissioned 11 large works.

During this time, Peter completed large canvases of Native peoples that were hung in the Luxton Museum. He drew pen and ink sketches for the public school's diplomas and completed a number of other paintings, sketches, and sculptures.

Writing about Peter's art, Paul and Shirley Swartz say, "By training Whyte was a traditionalist. He strove for accuracy. Just as he did not descend to sentimentalism, so neither did he impose an ideology upon his work. He was a painter, not a theorist, and one of Canada's finest."

On December 3, 1966, at the age of 61, Peter Whyte died peacefully in his sleep. His life had had its ups and downs. He had travelled the world, pursued his artistic talents, and shared these blessings with an enthusiastic and loving partner. He had touched many people through his stories, art, and benevolence. Sadly, he had wrestled in his final years with private demons and had not always triumphed. He is buried in Banff, the town he loved so dearly.

# Chapter 9
# The Wind in Her Sails

s the flight instructor left the plane, Catharine felt a twinge of apprehension. She was on her own. It was now time to summon all her courage, draw on all she had learned, and take off on a solo flight. Inspecting the gauges in the cockpit, wiping the sweat off her hands, and nodding over to the instructors who had helped her reach this point, Catharine's anxiety turned to excitement as she prepared for takeoff. On November 6, 1969, at the age of 63, Catharine received a certificate from the Chinook Flying School

to commemorate her first solo flight.

Gaining altitude and setting a new course were patterns for Catharine's golden years. Refusing to give up on life after Peter's death, Catharine had resolved to try new things and rekindle old passions. These years were some of the most active and daring of her life. Her appetite for learning was at its peak and she renewed her interest in skiing, painting, photography, and travel.

## Back to the Slopes

Skiing became Catharine's main recreational passion. The urge to ski again came after she watched the movie *Ski West*, which featured some 35-year-old film coverage of her Skoki days that had been shot by brother-in-law Cliff White. The choppy segments flashed from toothy grins and giddy horseplay, to shots of old friends skiing on alpine slopes. It had been more than 15 years since she had strapped skis to her feet so Catharine decided she needed a refresher course. She dragged her friend Maryalice Harvey Stewart along with her to the Norquay ski area. The first instructor they met was dismayed at the thought of taking two older women out on the slopes, so he passed the job off to Roy Andersen. Roy, a Norwegian instructor, was recognized as one of the most qualified instructors in the area. He delighted in the job. Catharine was keen and committed, and learned the new form of parallel skiing quickly. Their lessons became a regular occurrence, and their acquaintance grew into a close friendship.

Although Catharine never had her own children, she "adopted" children in her later years. Roy became like a son to her. He and his friends were frequent visitors to Catharine's home for steak dinners and après-ski parties. Roy shared his love of skiing and flying with Catharine. She was a supportive friend who helped him with his business endeavours.

For Christmas, a little more than one year after Peter died, Catharine used one of his skiing sketches as the design on her annual letter to friends and family. She explained her choice: "It [Peter's sketch] seems appropriate for after 20 years, learning to ski again … has meant more to me than anything else. It has opened up a new world of younger friends and new interests and given me more energy and enthusiasm."

Her ski lessons started on the nearby slopes of Norquay and Sunshine but Catharine also ventured to Europe to ski, and almost every year made at least one trip to British Columbia's Bugaboo Mountains. Her stamina was remarkable. One of Catharine's proudest accomplishments was winning the Senior Ladies' medal in a veterans ski race at the age of 71. She said it was the first medal she ever won and, rather uncharacteristically, she delighted in showing it to people.

**Patron of the Arts**
Throughout her life, Catharine wanted to aid people in reaching their fullest potential. When she was 18 years old she wrote in her journal, "The great question is what shall I do with my life and what one ought to do, whether to just try and be happy or make others happy. I think the latter way would do both." *Heritage Magazine* celebrated her success in 1976. It described Catharine as "always promoting interest in constructive causes, or support for imaginative projects, or backing for charitable undertakings ... [she] is the dynamo that quietly powers many a project, indicative of a warm heart and a great concern for her fellow Canadians." For many people, Catharine supplied the financial and emotional means to achieve their highest goals.

Music and the arts had always been important to Peter and Catharine. In 1966, Catharine met a 16-year-old violinist named David Zweifel. She was impressed with his talent and wanted to see him succeed. In an act that would have made her grandfather proud, Catharine helped pay his tuition at music school and partly financed his concert trips. She encouraged David's talent and urged him to strive to reach his potential. The two became great friends. Together, they climbed Mount Rundle and went on many ski trips. David stayed with Catharine in the summers while attending Master classes at The Banff Centre. As an adult, David moved to Europe and Catharine visited him and his wife in Switzerland. When he returned to Canada, Zweifel took a job with the Calgary Philharmonic Orchestra. Catharine delighted in David's musical abilities, and took a great interest in his career.

Catharine also supported one of Canada's foremost artistic organizations, The Banff Centre. Since the 1930s, The Banff Centre has been a place where budding and professional artists come to practice, and showcase their talent. She supported The Banff Centre's endeavours in spirit and in practice by serving on its board for many years. Also, Catharine used some of her inheritance money to help finance the construction of the institution's Margaret Greenham Theatre.

Sarain Stump was another young artist who benefited from Catharine's assistance. Sarain was the illustrator of a 1970 book called *There is My People Sleeping*, which had been published by Catharine and Peter's good friends Gray and Eleanor Campbell. Catharine was impressed by Sarain's work. She later purchased a number of his carvings, masks, and paintings for her home. Sarain headed the art department at the Indian Cultural College in Saskatchewan. He was one of the many talented native artists Catharine encouraged and promoted.

**Princess White Shield**

Catharine became a major financier of I.D.E.A.: Intercultural Development and Education through Art, a project established in 1968. The school was situated hundreds of kilometres away from Banff in northern Alberta, near Cold Lake. The project's goal was to help individuals learn more about art while fostering a sensitivity and respect for different cultures. More than 300 students of native, European, and other backgrounds attended the school. They produced paintings, ceramics, photographs, weaving, and other mixed media projects. Catharine funded art supplies and paid the teachers' salaries.

Catharine also maintained the Whyte family friendships in Morley. For years, she worked with Morley artists selling their handiwork, which she admired. Dressing up for special occasions, Catharine preferred beaded necklaces and leather medallions to diamonds and pearls. In the late 1960s, Catharine felt merchants in Banff were not paying native artisans enough for their art. She approached the Banff Chamber of Commerce about the issue, but nothing was done. In her own quiet way, she made a loud statement by buying all of the native art in Banff. With the help of the artists, Catharine set up the Alberta Stoney Indian Handicrafts business to sell the handiwork from her home. Catharine had her mother's keen business sense, which she shared with the native craftspeople. Later, the creators took over selling their own work.

At a powwow on Easter Monday in 1970, her Stoney friends officially honoured Catharine. At the ceremony, she was made a blood sister and given the name Princess White Shield. One of her oldest Canadian friends, Mary Kootenay of Morley, spearheaded a group who made a traditional, white buckskin dress for Catharine. The outfit featured geometric beaded designs and a fringe draped with beads. She was given a medallion 10 centimetres in diameter emblazoned with the image of a bison. It was the symbol of Walking Buffalo George McLean's family, of which she was now officially a member.

Three years later, the tribal administration made her an honorary chief of the Stoney Tribe in recognition of all the work she had done for their people.

## Culture and Conservation

Catharine's interest in travel peaked once again in her later years. In her sixties and seventies she took trips to Nepal, Europe, Asia, and Northern Canada. The trips were learning experiences that furthered her understanding of the need for preservation of undeveloped areas. She served as a trustee of the National and Provincial Parks Association. The conservation of cultural places and wild lands was one of Catharine's main concerns. She toured heritage sites and took part in meetings discussing the preservation of areas in northern Canada, British Columbia, the Bow Valley, and even the West Indies.

In July 1968, Catharine and her close friend Kathleen Daly Pepper set off for the cold climes of northern Canada. They travelled to an Inuit settlement called Povungnituk on the eastern side of Hudson Bay, just south of Baffin Island. Inspired by the faces of the people she met there, Catharine picked up her paintbrush, and her gift for portraiture was revived after a 30-year hiatus. After painting the distinctive features of one older Inuit woman,

Catharine found out her subject was the wife of Nanook, from the popular documentary *Nanook of the North.*

In 1970, Catharine was part of a group of hikers, climbers, Sherpas, and porters on an Alpine Club of Canada trip to the Himalayas. They trekked Nepal's high country, steep inclines, deep valleys, and dense forests, staying at friendly villages along the way. Surrounded by the world's highest peaks, they camped at spots thousands of metres above sea level. Many of her fellow hikers suffered from altitude sickness, but Catharine "was lucky and never missed a meal."

Catharine enjoyed travelling to places where there were indigenous people. Excursions of this kind took her to northern British Columbia, the Queen Charlotte Islands, South America, New Zealand, and Australia. The lush coastal forest and white rocky beaches of the Queen Charlotte Islands reminded Catharine of Maine. She delighted in learning more about the New Zealand Maori and Australian Aborigines and comparing and contrasting their cultures to other Pacific indigenous peoples from Hawaii and Canada.

Catharine returned to the tundra in 1974. This time she travelled with a group of 10 Banff high-school students. Jon Amatt, teacher and climber, led the group. They flew in to the Inuit village of Pangnirtung on Baffin Island. Catharine thought the desolate, rocky landscape and glacier-topped mountains beautiful. One day, after the rest of the group had set off on a hike, Catharine was alone in camp. She thought she would take advantage of the relatively warm weather of around 20 degrees Celsius. She walked to a nearby sandy beach and stripped down to take a dip, thinking to herself, "no bathing suit — no matter." She had scarcely entered the water before a low-flying passenger plane sailed overhead, putting a quick end to her skinny dip!

Catharine became close to the Inuit families she encountered in the north. With her usual ability to fit into any social setting, Catharine was invited to join a family as they left on a weeklong hunting trip. She slept on a caribou hide with the two little girls of the family, sharing household duties and responsibilities. One morning, she was wakened by a commotion outside her tent. The nearby water was ruby red and a beluga whale floated lifelessly alongside the hunters' boats. Everyone got a strip of whale meat before they packed up and headed for home.

A mutual concern for the preservation of the world's cultures deepened a friendship with Jim

Thorsell of Banff. They travelled together to visit proposed conservation sites in Canada and the West Indies. One of Catharine's last trips was to the lush, tropical island of Dominica where she visited Jim, who was helping to develop a national park. Her travelling companion was her nephew Jon Whyte. Catharine was close to all her nieces and nephews, but she and Jon shared many of the same interests. The two also travelled to Asia together in 1977. Her travelogue of their trip to Asia recounts their adventures in Japan, Russia, and Afghanistan.

Despite a busy schedule of world travel, Catharine enjoyed returning to Banff. She delighted in the company of her family and friends — Banff had truly become home. She supported the town in many ways, often anonymously. She cared about this small mountain town Peter had brought her to so many years before, and wanted to see its citizens prosper and its culture and landscape preserved.

Catharine received all kinds of awards and commendations for her participation and support of various causes. In 1969, she was presented with an Honorary Doctorate from the University of Calgary and was named Outstanding Citizen of the Year by the Banff Kiwanis Club. In 1975, she received the Alberta Achievement Award, followed by the Award of Merit from the Historical Society of Alberta in 1978. Her highest honour came in that same year, when she was chosen for the Order of Canada. Catharine accepted all the honours bestowed upon her with characteristic modesty.

She never stopped exploring the Rocky Mountain trails. One fall day, while hiking a trail at Lake O'Hara, Catharine noticed a glob of paint on the bark of a yellowing larch tree. Instantly, she was transported back in time to her first summer in Banff when she and Peter were painting with the famous artist, J .E. H. MacDonald. MacDonald customarily wiped extra paint onto the bark of trees. Here was a cluster of paint more than 40 years old — a reminder of a love that had consumed her, days spent outside, and a life well lived. Catharine peeled the paint off the bark and took it home. It sits today beside her favourite vase by a sunny, north-facing window.

At the age of 72, Catharine Whyte passed away after complications from cancer. In memory of his aunt, Jon Whyte placed a larch branch in her favourite cobalt blue and apple green vase that sat on her windowsill at home. The branch still serves as a reminder of her gracious spirit, the lives she touched, and the generosity she showed others.

## Chapter 10
# A Lasting Legacy

A warm breeze tickled the long grasses near the Morley reservation where Peter, Catharine, and their friend Walking Buffalo George McLean were comfortably seated. It was a summer day in the late 1950s, and the three were musing on a name for the foundation the couple wanted to establish. "Wa-Che-Yo-Cha-Pa" was the name the medicine man offered. Explaining his choice, he said the phrase meant, "anything you see, anything you do, it's perfect. Doesn't matter what you do or what you see. All there. Would draw influence … in that way perfect, in that way nice and beautiful. Your mind draws to the work, and the influence draws. Can't say nothing against." The name fit.

The Whytes' foundation had a name. Later, after explaining its meaning to a number of people, Catharine and her nephew David Stockand, a journalist, paraphrased McLean's phrase to: "Where the good, the wise, and the beautiful come together in harmony." It was a tenet that would guide Peter and Catharine's dream to construct a multi-faceted community building that would include a library, archives, art gallery, and public space for performances. The idea had been percolating since the early 1940s. Catharine's brother Russell, who acted as her financial advisor throughout her life, was the first to suggest that she and Peter set up a foundation to manage the financial aspects of supporting such cultural endeavours. The Whytes' passion for learning and sharing cultural experiences naturally melded into a dream of providing a resource building of this sort for their own community.

Initially, Peter and Catharine thought that their dream would come to fruition after they had passed on. They had designated funds in their will to be used to develop a local museum for Banff residents and its visitors. However, after Peter's death, these plans moved ahead. Catharine began working with an enthusiastic promoter of the project, the acting town archivist Maryalice Harvey Stewart. Maryalice was a spitfire with a strong vision and the drive to help make Catharine's dream a reality. Another factor in moving the dream ahead was Canada's quickly approaching Centennial, giving a timeframe for the completion of the project.

In 1967, construction began on the $500,000 building that would house an archive, library, art gallery, and public performance space. The building was erected on the Whytes' property, nestled between their home, the town's Central Park, and the Bow River. Just a block off Banff Avenue, at the end of Bear Street, the building was located in the heart of Banff. Philip Delasalle of the Calgary architectural firm Cohos, Delasalle and Evamy designed the 1400-square-metre building. He used materials that would blend in with the natural environment, including the same stone used to build the Banff Springs Hotel, cedar wood, and earth-coloured paint. The building was reinforced with concrete and had fireproof walls to protect its collections.

The library and archives were housed on the main level of the building. When the building opened, the library consisted of a collection of approximately 10,000 books. There were cosy rugs on the floor of the children's area to accommodate youngsters reading in whatever position felt most comfortable. The interior of the library was designed to be as welcoming as possible for locals, summer staff, and visitors. The archives consisted of historical photographs, newspapers, brochures, private collections of correspondence and documents, and other artifacts that were associated with the region. Stocked by local donations and organized under Maryalice's watchful eye, the goal of the archives was to preserve the history of the Rocky Mountain's pioneers, Native peoples, and townsfolk. Downstairs, the Peter Whyte Gallery was part of an area suitable for public performances such as films, lectures, and readings. The first exhibit in the gallery was a showing of more than 100 of Peter Whyte's sketches and oil paintings. It was a fitting tribute to one of the building's benefactors.

On Sunday June 16, 1968, two of Banff's legends, sculptor and cowboy artist Charlie Beil, and celebrated outfitter Jimmy Simpson were on hand to declare the new building open. They spoke to a crowd of more than 500 onlookers. Jimmy called attention to Catharine and thanked her for donating the institution to the people and visitors of Banff. Then, he cut through a buckskin cord, officially opening the Banff Public Library and Archives of the Canadian Rockies.

Catharine Whyte, the institution's prime supporter — the person who, through her vision and financial gifts, made the building a possibility — stood quietly in the background. She looked elegant and stately in a pencil skirt and dark blouse with a corsage pinned to her left lapel. Her grandest feature that day was the smile she wore as she shook hands with the people who had helped make her dream a reality. Peter was there in spirit, with his sketches and oil paintings on display in the art gallery.

# Epilogue

In many ways, Peter and Catharine Whyte were quintessential Banff residents. Their two strongest passions, art and nature, were combined with a deep care that they be preserved for future generations. Their integrity and ambition culminated in the building of what is now known as the Whyte Museum of the Canadian Rockies.

Peter and Catharine's door is still open for visitors from all over the world as part of the museum. This heritage home's intrigue remains although its inhabitants are gone. Their generous spirit lives on in the memories of those who knew them, in the letters they wrote, the paintings they created, the artistic lure of Banff, and their crowning achievement — a museum and archive that celebrate human endeavour and nature. Their lives touched many people through their commitment to the past, delight in the present, and hope for the future.

# Bibliography

Christensen, Lisa. *A Hiker's Guide to Art of the Canadian Rockies*. Calgary: Fifth House, 1999.

Hart, E. J. *The Place of Bows: Exploring the Heritage of the Banff-Bow Valley*. Banff: EJH Literary Enterprises Ltd., 1999.

Hutchings, Sebastian. *Banff: An Altitude SuperGuide*. Canmore: Altitude Publishing, 2002.

Manry, Kathryn. *Skoki: Beyond the Passes*. Calgary: Rocky Mountain Books, 2001.

Whyte, Jon. Editor. *Catharine Robb Whyte and Peter Whyte: A Commemorative Portfolio*. Banff: The Peter and Catharine Whyte Foundation, 1980.

Whyte, Jon. *Indians in the Rockies*. Canmore: Altitude Publishing Ltd., 1985.

Whyte, Jon and Edward Cavell. *Mountain Glory: the Art of Peter and Catharine Whyte.* Banff: Whyte Museum of the Canadian Rockies, 1988.

The following sources were also used in the research of this book:

"Art Displays Many and Varied," *Banff Crag and Canyon*, August 19, 1949.

"Call of the Canyon," *Banff Crag and Canyon*, October 3, 1952.

"Catharine Whyte Remembered," *Banff Crag and Canyon*, June 20, 1979.

"Library, Archives Building for Banff," *Banff Crag and Canyon*, August 16, 1967.

"New Archives Building on Bear Street Open Sunday," *Banff Crag and Canyon*. June 12, 1968.

Peter and Catharine Whyte Fonds. M36/S37/V683. Whyte Museum of the Canadian Rockies.

"Peter Whyte — the War Years," *Banff Crag and Canyon*, June 22, 1977.

Swartz, Dr. Paul and Shirley. "Peter Whyte" in Arts West. Volume 1, Number 6. 1976, pp. 12–15.

# Acknowledgments

I would like to thank the helpful staff at the Whyte Museum of the Canadian Rockies, especially Lena Goon, Elizabeth Kundert-Cameron, and Carol Mowat. My sincere appreciation to Archivist Don Bourdon and Ted Hart of the Peter and Catharine Whyte Foundation. Thank you to the Whytes for their lasting legacy in the Bow Valley. I am grateful to everyone at Altitude Publishing and editor Lauri Seidlitz. Thanks to Roy Andersen and Jon Whelan for the insights, and Jennifer Lee and Bill Snider for the compassion. Hugs to all the Write-On sisters. Mandi Kujawa, thanks for the "ra-ra." Love to Mom, Dad, Missy, and Kevin and my supportive circle of friends and family.

The author wishes to acknowledge that the quotations and photographs contained in this book are reproduced courtesy of the Whyte Museum of the Canadian Rockies, Peter and Catharine Whyte Fonds. M36/S37/V683.

# About the Author

Kim Mayberry lives, works, writes, and plays in Canmore, Alberta with her husband Kevin, and dog Denali. She freelances for local newspapers and magazines. This is her first book. She enjoys the beauty of the mountains, but sometimes misses the wide prairie skies over the farm outside of Red Deer where she grew up.

# OTHER AMAZING STORIES

These titles are available wherever you buy books. If you have trouble finding the book you want, call the Altitude order desk at 1-800-957-6888, e-mail your request to: orderdesk@altitudepublishing.com or visit our Web site at www.altitudepublishing.com.

All titles retail for $9.95 Cdn or $7.95 US.
(Prices subject to change.)

New Amazing Stories titles are constantly being published. If you would like to be informed when new titles are available, e-mail your name and mailing address to: amazingstories@altitudepublishing.com.